Green Burial

Green Burial

poems

DEREK GRAF

ELIXIR PRESS
Denver, Colorado

Cover design by Valentin Manov

Library of Congress Cataloging-in-Publication Data

Names: Graf, Derek, author.
Title: Green burial : poems / Derek Graf.
Description: First edition. | Denver, Colorado : Elixir Press, [2023]
Identifiers: LCCN 2022020621 | ISBN 9781932418798 (paperback)
Subjects: LCGFT: Poetry.
Classification: LCC PS3607.R3289 G74 2023 | DDC 811/.6--dc23/
eng/20220502
LC record available at https://lccn.loc.gov/2022020621

ISBN: 978-1-932-41879-8

First edition: TK

10   9   8   7   6   5   4   3   2   1

Table of Contents

Green Burial

Genesis Litany

In the beginning I pulled this bullet from a coyote's stomach.

In the beginning only the wind made us possible.

In the beginning she slept in a room overrun with the infinite traffic of
ants.

In the beginning we reached the limits of our vocabulary.

In the beginning there was a boy perched in the branches of a redwood two
hundred feet in the air.

In the beginning, he says, these words looked just like rain.

*

Sacrifice Zones

Low buildings stacked like pallets
in a warehouse. The rain's seeking
safe passage and she's been dead

two years now. Low buildings,
safe rain, how will we survive the night?
Someone sets fire to the wire

fences bordering the oil refinery.
My body hurts everywhere
and everywhere it hurts to breathe.

Small Continuous Explosions

That was the night my lover hit rock bottom.

Drove her truck off the road into a cattle pasture.

Ants smothered in white vinegar scatter along the patio ledge.

I need to give up my obsession with endings.

Flocks of oil-stained cranes drowning in the Atlantic.

She chokes back a bottle of wine on the drive to rehab.

Then she's gone, dragged dead drunk in the arms of orderlies.

That was the night the artery burst in her brain.

Her words erupt like small, continuous explosions inside me.

Her father stands at the birdbath in his backyard until dawn.

I take off my clothes limb by limb. *Drink this*, she said. And I did.

Forms of Interiority

A body falls
            through the galaxies
inside an opal.

A body falls
            on a mattress
after working all night
            at a construction site.

In this industrial forest,
            every cell of your body
dissipates into vapor.

We were united
            in our solitude, recalling
the dead eyes of horses
            smothered in toxins

at the rendering plant:
            looking away, staring back.

Deep Time

1/

Darwin sketches his portrait
to forget about God. My lover cleans flesh

from the skull of a bobcat.

By candlelight, Darwin glances over
his aging shoulder.

I wait in the free clinic for hours,
surrendered to the present tense.

2/

As I drive away from my brother's funeral,

Darwin scans his notes for inaccuracies,
slips of logic. Tonight, he wants

to write about causality and survival.

My brother drags heavy
furniture down the driveway
on his last morning alive.

I wade through the present tense
of my own organism, waiting

for the right words.

Vibrant Matter

Listen: we are in the midst of the ragged human

process of breathing. Following the atomic

clock, I throw glass bottles in the dumpster

behind my apartment. When I peel back the layers

of my failing body, the unearthed light of morphine

floods this room. People recycle themselves in the warm

refrain of open windows. The sun collapses and dies.

Manual for Living

You can leap to heaven from the dump.

You can give up on your words before they become speech.

Listen: snowdrifts lean over the highway like headlines.

In the back of the white van she says, *I miss the old you.*

We walk to the tree only to realize we forgot the rope.

An entire religion backpedals into the hills.

We leave the van in the field with the tree: a reunion of ordered things.

The branches shake in the language of the way home.

To My Dead Neighbor

Not even the phrase makes sense:
a dead neighbor is no neighbor
at all, according to one dictionary.
I'm sorry I'm not home much
these days, shifting from lane
to lane across highways far
removed from here, my apartment,
where I write to you tonight,
and only tonight, dead man.

There is no foreseeable future.
Our rent stays the same, your story
disappears from the local paper.
How many nights has it been
since you last poured an ounce
of clear rum into that shot glass
you picked up in, what was it, Paris?

Listen: young couples lean
into each other at the jazz bar
downtown, and the night permits
all this without you, absent you.
From the morning news, I learn
that three out of every twenty
children will suffer a serious injury
while riding the school bus.
And just last week, everyone
in the mall looked over
their shoulder when the dumpster
exploded out back. If the day
persists, our plumbing
will work without a hitch.

The heat radiates effortlessly,
natural light pierces through
all the bedroom windows.

But when the bearded man
across the hall starts shouting
motherfucker and *shithead*
at his giant television,
kicking the door as though
he were trapped forever
in this square footage we call home,
I will think of you, the quiet
kind, the sort of person who dies
quietly, and three weeks later
still receives handfuls
of credit card bills, some junk-mail.

A Material World

Another foreclosed home, another family forced onto the lawn under a low-lying Florida sun. Incessant light peels away the cheap paint of patio chairs. The downtown streets are quiet. All the storefronts locked up. The tumor on my brother's brain swells in his sleep. At dawn the sky is asphalt runoff. By afternoon, halting blue. We are contingent, conditioned. Listen: children dive into the community pool all weekend. The water's so cold they come up screaming.

Were I Castor, the Poem I'd Write Pollux

would be my body

and its only sound, though its only sound
hums incomplete, the way

words between lovers become
words the dead write with their tongues.

Pollux, your voice is not my voice—
my voice is a slow silence crawling

from earth back to earth, where rain
is our only parable—but even

as children you refused the frail animal
in my lesser blood. Pollux, let us begin

this autopsy of *one*, as one
sparrow alights inside your godhead.

Through the fogged tides
I watch children release sailboats

of paper and tape. When I ask
for their names my voice chokes on reeds.

Better Weather

Stockyards and streetlights. Abandoned apartments.

Gutted storefronts, coke lines, stop signs. Humidity

and corrosion and rust. We take asylum in naked

diction: she says the rain's fading—I say it's fading

everywhere. What's the point of healing? Covering

her body with mine to stall our rupturing? We have

lungs, a little cash, crowded bars, and steel pipes

to shatter each streetlight: daily ruins born of unrest

and weak ambition like smoke inside a prison.

Getting By

Like a thread of birds. Their identical eyes. Like the canal we watch dry up
all summer.

I open another book, remember her throwing her shoulder against the door.

I remember her fugitive days: fidgeting for a smoke halfway through group
therapy.

Wasting away, disappearing. The identical eyes of strangers smothering her
only window.

My hands regret to remember her. She trims the wick of every candle in her
room.

Abundant Scarcity

The dumpster piles up all day
       and then tilts over.

Let us forget our names—
       they were never spoken.

In the hospital parking lot
       a man with a bleeding arm collapses.

So many animals devour one another,
       I've forgotten how to keep count.

Scarce Abundance

We know our garbage
        by its smell, beautiful

and certain to disgust.
        The pipes are frozen,

water tinged with rust.
        Street dogs of irreverent

hunger crowd the dumpster.
        I pay off my medical bills

in minor installments
        of empty promises.

Every morning the hot
        water gives out before

I'm even naked: beautiful
        and certain to disgust.

The Always Diversion

After she died I could no longer imagine
deer huddled in the shaded greenways
of the back country. Or clouds brawling
into afternoon storms, the lake overrunning
our neighborhood streets. Everything became
literal: brown horses, men painting houses
all summer, a bowl of white rice. In the end
she was just another rehab story. In the end
I picked up the patio furniture she'd thrown
over the ledge the night before. Turns out
we were only brief particles in a world
smothered with particles: useless matter.

Rain sweeps over the backyard like a heist.
I make dinner in total silence. Fruit flies
swarm over the kitchen sink. As night falls
I walk into the wet grass and I'm young
again, a body of fresh particles stepping
solidly into the world. I breathe for what
must be the first time, imagine her
leading me somewhere shaded, new.

This Close

We stand at the doors of her childhood home.

Hungry for metaphors, the bruised branches of June

point toward nothing. All summer the lunatic petals

of the dogwood shrubs are this close to beautiful.

I'm trying to stay sober as the owl that waits up

all night for its next meal. She sleeps inside the canyon

of my failing heart. The doorway dims, gleams.

Analog Pastoral

Valley winds echo

through the fields
of our conversation.

All night the town's

drummer stays up
tightening his skins.

What green betrays:

the trees give up
their obsession

with the wind. Every
day, bright surfaces.

On the bright surface
of every day, one small

river resembles another.

I sleep in identical towns
under a thousand names,

aching to feel different.

Digital Pastoral

History rushes toward us
in the guise of a rave.

I sleep in websites
incorrectly coded, holding
for customer support.

We stumble through
a synthesis of tangled wires,
raving and broken-hearted.

We visit towns smothered
in death-threats, searching

for the man who changed
the name of every insect
to *pest*. We find him

wading in a barrel
of crude oil: our termite hearts
gripped in his slick fingers.

The Chemicals in Our Veins Speak in Pleasant Voices, While

mournful sounds seep out from pried-open elevator doors.

A brutal accident, someone says on the evening news.

Herds of cattle huddle against summer's incalculable sum.

Old men stare into the passage of real water, all their faces comatose.

I hear the braying of a mule nearby, locked up and starving in a barn.

The skyline is a brutal accident of glass and concrete.

A black car backfires. Helicopters linger over transmission towers.

The oxygen here is so thick it smothers our tongues.

Every premise is an eviction of another premise, a scarring.

A city appears in the teeth of a breaking wave.

I can't afford a new face. Wait: I can afford a new face if you will buy my old one.

Her body breaks down into lithic fragments, whatever we call earth.

The Patient on the Dump

When I dream of the landfill, I wake organic and new.

Prosthetic hearts and plastic bottles surround me

like children. It is blissful. It is blissful to strip off

this hospital gown and glide through the desert.

All my symptoms skip town into someone else's body.

When I wash up on the Colorado with my whole life

before me, the sun sets in real time. In real time,

the setting sun breaks my prosthetic heart.

Less Science More Junk

I cough so hard I spit up

geometry. Lights in the clinic

bright as a teenager's dress

on prom night. One day

I'll be the implied narrator

of my life story: *His mouth*

resembled an exhaust pipe.

Outside my window the river

aches like a failing light bulb.

You're the third stranger in a row

who's said to me: *Water is life.*

When I look inside my stomach

I see a riot of science and junk.

At birth we're commissioned

to reach out and touch everything.

There's a word for the company

I keep. It sounds nothing like *earth*.

Earthly Reminders

I memorize the names of European cities

from glossy postcards tacked

on my bedroom wall. My brother

holds the table while a small earthquake

ruptures another morning. The oil derrick

maintains the reliable atmospherics

of our suburban homestead. She calls me

from rehab, begging for a ride home.

Some anonymous survey wants to know

where I stand in the most literal sense.

Most days I wait around for bread

to rise in the oven. Most days I pretend

I live in a postcard. No one notices

how I'm floating away all the time,

unmoored from the sounds

of words I never really understood.

The Hotel in Shreveport

She wakes up in the thick moss of the Gulf of Mexico.

She wakes up standing around an open grill

with a Coors Light in her hand. I want a new year

and a new city and a new body. A steel pipe in the television.

We rip down the deer skull mounted on her father's office wall.

She kicks the mound of aluminum cans at her feet.

Her kiss: it's like popping blisters inside my tongue.

Sometimes I walk for so long I can't remember my name.

She finds love smoking Marlboros at a hotel in Shreveport.

I wake up at noon with my fist in the television.

There Is No Punishment That Does Not Purify

I nailed my audition for the snuff film.
It's streaming everywhere.

You can watch it on your laptop
as you lie in bed clipping your toenails.

You can clip your toenails and watch
some hooded figure stab me in the stomach.

Don't tell anyone, but the hooded
figure is me. I'm the one who kills me.

Don't tell anyone, but in the movie
I have a tattoo on my back. It says:

there is no punishment that does not purify.

Health and Vandalism

She throws a handle of vodka against the wall
to announce that the fight is over.

We all believe we're alone, running from bridge
to bridge without notice.

No one thinks she's worth the trouble
once they boil her down to a small country of facts.

She sends everyone she knows a text with her last words,
but forgets the hard truth that dreams should bring.

All day I walk down streets where I'm nothing
more than an algorithm of shirts.

The moon broods like it was born in dirt.
She swears no one dies fighting off temptation anymore.

The facts are obvious, the bedroom goes dark.

In Every Hypothetical

When I leap from the rooftop garden

of the Midwest Bank building,

my bones shatter like the dishes

you threw at my face

when you were too drunk

to look at me. Love, in every hypothetical

I forgive you. On these nights

when even the moon's falling

fast, I see myself rising from that crowded,

blood-soaked sidewalk to promise you this:

I will never go anywhere.

Descent of Man

Darwin drags me down a staircase and feasts.
On my guts. Feasts. With his startling teeth.

The sky above us is pale green.
The sky above us is always pale green.

He washes my blood off his black leather boots.
Rips every painting to shreds before I prime the canvas.

He understands crude tools, blunt instruments,
and territorial grunts. He hates art unless it deadens him.

No children stalk his brutal heart. In his brutal heart,
an orchestra swells over a pile of horse bones.

Darwin drags me into a culvert and feasts.
Like a dog. One hungry fucking dog.

Special Effects

Dust clouds of blasted concrete. The interior of the moon.

My mother drives to the cemetery through fields battered with wind.

A stretch of ice-tongued trees.

Inside my father there is another father with his hand on my shoulder.

I write him down the way worms cling to the earth.

The car rushes over potholes the county will never fill in.

Compressions of space and time. Anonymous planets of water, sand.

My body passes through the doors of a stranger's bedroom.

The tide falls a little shorter every day. That's how death works.

Like being pushed out of a room you used to sleep in.

Invisible forces, special effects. The car rising over the fields.

Last Street in the South

Someone hangs nooses around the city all summer:

tethered to the doors of chapels, schools, the state capitol.

Last night three children were left for dead on the fire escape

of my apartment building. Two men lean against the white

concrete walls of a bowling alley, beers in their hands, staring down

everyone who drives past. *Won't You Spare One Dollar for Jesus?*

All I know is this place I call home sinks into the ocean too slowly.

Local History

A gym towel heavy with another man's sweat.

If I had a body without this local history,

without countless identical examples,

perhaps then I could say something new.

Now my tongue swells with the sound of her name,

and the day hangs from a coat-hook. Ignore it,

I tell myself. Ignore the locust trees

and the burn-pit in your mouth:

remember her hands on your back, her tongue

in your ear, her name waxing down your spine.

Apocryphal Dirt

There's another me wandering through the lobby.

On television, poisonous gas billows from a pulpit.

We sleep on benches dedicated to dead men.

The night porter tries to drink himself to death.

The night porter tells me I should stay in school.

I fall asleep in the future perfect, wake up there too.

Listen: the landfill pulls me in like a lecture.

The apocryphal history of dirt covers my thumbnail.

I hear my name buried in its verbs.

No Birds

In the next stage of human evolution,
we'll all be able to afford our groceries,
medical bills, abortions, and antiviral
prescriptions. The next stage
of human evolution will arrive
in the form of paid-in-full insurance
premiums, complimentary dental exams,
marriage counseling, and oil changes.

There are no birds in my house.
But as humans evolve into creatures
actually beautiful there might be
two birds or three birds in my house.

And when the evolutionary narrative
of human life begins a new chapter,
every morsel of dirt I have collected
under my fingernails will flush toward
the drain as I stand naked
in my very own shower, in my home
that has no rent or mortgage.
Every loan is already approved
in the next stage of human evolution.
Prepare your house for the birds.

Contemporania

My interpretation of the animal is weakening.

Tomorrow the sea (even the *inland* sea).

In a word, emerging celestial bodies.

That's it: at the end of this sentence I will carve out something real.

A remix of your favorite track. The picture of your stagnant face.

Our historical moment spits blood onto the sidewalk.

The act of coming or going. The overexposed negative.

You were my contemporary in the hour before I blacked out.

I set my boundaries like a screensaver (this is the hour when you transgress them).

We slide down the dunes of our present tense. Saying nothing, feeling feelings.

Obscenity Trial

She buries her hands in the wet reeds

of my hair. In this eclipsed light

I can't recognize her face. She passes

through the drowned room. Says,

we don't know our limits. Black clouds spill

from concrete towers, chemical plants issue muscles

of smoke across the Atlantic, and the lightbulb

burns a geological age across her sleeping face.

Cars line the motel parking lot like a military front.

Bricks in windshields, arson across town.

I turn the deadbolt: her face shines through

the deep map of motel sheets. Charred daylight

claws against her closed eyes. Morning: bright radio static.

The furious light of a muted television. Our shadows a riot of limbs.

The sun rises over the landfill. Someone cries out

we are starved we are starved. Six weeks sober, a new grammar crashes against the shores of my mouth. Cash and chemical

clouds drift over the Atlantic. Sleep crests over us like oil

running down coastal rocks. She buries her hand

in the withered garden of my hand.

Super 8

I turn the light back on and ask
if you're asleep now.

Vast trains over brief miles
and tomorrow isn't even here yet.

Deviant Materials

Deep in the lexicon of rural America,

farmers plunder their homes for firewood.

Fields slope downward into green distances.

At the dump, blades of grass needle

upward through rubber and plastic.

Every billboard along the highway draws me

closer to a landfill where waste takes new form.

The fence posts collapse like pill bottles tossed

down a toilet. Trees fall crashing against other trees.

Super 8 Revisited

These are the hours that curl
from our mouths like syllables

forced into the wrong words
I said when you were asleep then.

What did I say? Prayer for the moon
to pull us through vacant days, prayer

for evening trains, the night's pure
arc, these alleys where the dark slings

its body over shallow puddles and trash.

The Enabler Explains Himself

She walks home from the party reeling like bad camerawork.

Someone's husband made her a drink in the laundry room.

I throw a scarf over the lampshade to see myself in a different light.

My hands withdraw inside my hands. The sheet clings to her like a simile.

Spreading soap on my skin, I call myself a real bastard.

When her corpse revives at the funeral, I throw my tuxedo in a garbage bag.

Three aspirin later, she sleeps like a used anthology. Like a dropped course.

This is a matter of death and death. A scarf in the middle of summer.

The Organic Principle of Extinction, Part 1:
Almost Human

We were converted into plastic
        and told we would live forever.
We copied your vices, voices.
        Wore imperfect, smothering flesh.
We breathed your troubled
        oxygen through artificial lungs.

We purchased expensive cosmetics
        to look like you. We took lovers
and luxurious meals. We knew
        how to act natural. Sit and wait.
Stare through windows. Speak.

We never wanted to live forever.
        Struck no bargain. Made no plans.
The last days of humanity arrived
        and we mimicked your mass death.
We cried and pretended to pray.

        It seemed natural we should die
along with you. We were certain
        no one would see the difference.

Ordinary Moon

Winter starts with a brick through her windshield.

In her hands, wet leaves. In the wet leaves, the bones

of an owl. We tried our best and still failed to flesh

each other out. She's drunk and the moon is ordinary.

My neighbor across the alley is sleeping, visible

and invisible behind half-drawn curtains.

Winter shaves away another hour of sunlight

like a thousand men leaning over a sink.

We haven't slept a night through in weeks.

When I talk about her I forget I'm talking

about myself. Listen, she says, there's no one left

to listen. She waits for me and takes what she needs.

A drink, a bed. A familiar body to fall against.

Rehab Story

Jeffrey thinks the birdbath is a baptismal pool.

Katherine waits in the parking lot for her son.

I'm sure I don't know the difference between love and guilt.

In certain lights there's a serial number on my tongue.

The glare of aluminum foil. The ashtray on the windowsill.

We clean plastic bowls covered in oatmeal and chocolate milk.

Eddie talks about the day the sun will explode.

The last thing to do, he says, is rechristen every continent.

The sun disappears as I walk to my room.

You don't see the hospital if you only look at the grounds.

Dumpster Birds

They tear through plastic bags
        in the gutters of frontage roads.
No one remembers
        that they were once beautiful.

The windshields in morning gridlock
        glisten like gold in an open vault.

They fly past stalled-out vehicles
        with abandon, landing among crumbs
of blueberry muffins, potato skins.

They persist beyond the conclusion
        of all narrative, croaking
that every prophet is a false prophet
        in the parking lot of the outlet mall.

The night dissolves into deadened
        hours. They go hungry, sleep little.
One thin cloud hovers over them
        in the shape of an open beak.

Last Call

In another drunk text she promised

to slit her wrists and leave her body

on the bathroom floor. She wanted me

to find her like that, an act we rehearsed

nightly. Waiting outside her apartment

for an hour with no answer, I almost

believed her. I sat there revisiting

all the nights she looked for someone

to walk her home after last call,

after the vodka tonics and hundred-dollar tabs.

The look on her face when she wouldn't wake up

no matter how hard I shook her. The hospital

lobbies I waited in until dawn. All the nights

I refused to stay with her—I can't say

who was more afraid of the other:

was I certain she'd mistake my body

and mouth for someone else? I imagined her

stumbling out of the bar, almost falling against

the jukebox, pushing aside everyone in her way.

She appeared in the alley of her apartment building

hours later, too drunk to remember why

I was there, or the promises we both failed to keep.

The Organic Principle of Extinction, Part 2: Better Than Any Orgasm

How tired we were by the world's end.
    How sick of predictions, furious omens.

The relief we felt when the soot-smothered
    clouds surrounded us was total.

Someone said it felt better than any orgasm.
    Many nodded. It was the end of history

for real this time: we had to forfeit our bones.

Someone said it was more than death
    we were experiencing. Someone said,

this is experience itself. When I was absorbed
    by the eruptions and high flames,

I forgot everyone's name, all the reasons why
    I might have said: You mean the world to me.

Love and Theft and the Airport

She's got clean white sneakers and no prior models

for a healthy relationship. She's bothered by voices

over the phone. She's bothered by voices in real life

too, especially her own. At the airport I tell her

We're not right for each other and she says *Who is?*

Everything we know about ourselves was stolen

years ago. I crush one ant on the counter

and notice twenty more in the sink. On television,

someone identical to her crawls out from beneath

a burning plane. I wash mushrooms again and again,

she watches me drown inside her hands. And one day,

the pain in my stomach disappears as I watch her cut up

her credit cards. We contain no borders, no boundaries:

sincere dishonesty awaits us. Another sinkhole opens

while we sleep, swallowing everyone identical to us.

Ecosexual Fantasy

That's us having sex during the tour of the rendering plant.

Naked on the floor, bodies coated with lard and oil.

An orgy of feathers and hair and grease.

This is the dirtiest job in America, the tour guide says.

Bone and marrow, blood and tallow. Barrels, conveyer belts.

When you came I remembered what it means to have a body.

What it means to live and die and breathe and bleed. To pulse.

La petite mort, or something. My guts are the meat I've been fed.

The tour guide explains the evolution of soap and wax and glue.

Your scent still clings to my skin. That's how I know you'll live again.

Eye Contact

My body double orbits this dry January.

All our friends are drunk again. I turn

off the lights in the high school music room

every night for a decade. What was it I tried

to say? In the rear-view mirror I watch

my body double avert his eyes and waste away.

A State of Suspension

I'm most alive when I pass a razor down my throat.

All in the name of hygiene. In the name of paradise.

Hey wait a minute! someone shouts at the statue covered in pigeon shit.

My sponsor tells me to forgive this bankrupt version of myself.

A state of suspension, always waiting for test results.

You know you're having a good time when you can reach in and touch your
pulse.

All my organs are subject to copyright laws. Forever trademarked, patented.

When it comes to a good time nothing is out of the question.

In paradise there are no children except the children of paradise.

They Don't Tell You That the Pursuit of Happiness Leads to Sorrow

In my dream she was Jacques Demy
    and I was Agnès Varda. In my dream

she was dead and I was making films
    about her. The beaches here are nameless

and the visitors, very strange. Her father
    said that in her eyes there was still a little life.

She told me it was snowing in New England—
    a place she had never been. No one around

here seems to know what the clouds sound like.
    I want to write her a letter containing

every thought that passes through my mind.
    She told me I should keep a notebook.

I will call it *The New England Notebook.*

The Organic Principle of Extinction, Part 3: Alternate Ending

The good news is the helicopters
have arrived. The bad news
is they aren't taking everyone.
Pallets of foodstuffs and toiletries
clutter the jet-bridge. Austere men
with automatic rifles smoke the last
cigarettes of the twenty-first century.

Is this really how we're going out?
Everything was a lie. There were millions
of years to prepare for this
and we waited until all the birds
had plummeted from the pale green sky.

The woman I love has run away.
The man I love has taken refuge
in a grocery store. The bad news
is the water: poisonous
and in short supply. The good news
is I don't have to worry anymore
about the most painful way to die.

Houses Filled with People Who Resemble Other People

Every painting in this museum

draws me back to the border

between Texas and Oklahoma:

strung-out, broke-down, walking

down gravel alleys in a dry county.

Cockroaches crawling across

rust stains in the bathtub, that's what

I remember about the motel

in Ardmore. You were a swarm

of events and I was a shoveled creek.

I was a highway's dream and you

were a taste of earth. That's what

I remember, anyway. I won't say

it was a painting that made me

think of you again, that pulled me

into wondering why we were never

married or sober. I spend my days

in houses filled with people who resemble

other people. A few of them I miss.

A few of them I'll never see again.

The One You Like the Most

For all I know, the lights
           are judged for seeping.

There's harm in asking
           where you're from.

I keep two crutches
           and one broken lamp

in my closet. Look,
           the steam pipes walk

right into the street
           before they explode,

and the crowd goes wild.
           You thought you'd last

forever until you grew
           senile about the river.

I found you under
           the ground in a troubled

niche. There's no harm,
           I'm certain, mangling

a cloud, and I know I just
           know I will see you again.

Green Burial

Tonight the trees are paper
nuns leaning over fox bones.

And I'm still here.

Near the railroad cars,
the shallow hillside.

My bones as brittle as dry soil.

*

      Give me your glass-eyed stare.
Ask me if these graves have any use at all.

Tonight, we are just as designed
for flight as a rhythm of sparrows,

our wings severed

in artificial light. Look:
this nest is bleeding.

*

Why do my eyes mistake the chapel
     for a mound of bones, bright as it is?

Nothing moves beneath the trees.

And the trees are so still—I doubt

           they are even real.

*

Apocalypse Litany

In the end all the oil derricks could finally sleep.

In the end your face grew dim and shapeless and secret.

In the end our bodies were deemed sacrifice zones.

In the end they laid you down in a casket made of particleboard.

In the end we left the boy stranded in the branches of a redwood two hundred feet in the air.

In the end my father found me wandering among moss-smothered trees in the swamps of Florida.

In the end this conversation broke down into doubtful flames.

Acknowledgements

This book would not exist without the guidance and support of many friends, family members, and colleagues. Among them are my former professors, Katie Riegel, Jay Hopler, Lisa Lewis, Trey Moody, and Rose McLarney. Megan Kaminski, who saw this manuscript through many drafts during my time at the University of Kansas, has been a constant source of encouragement and wisdom.

I am equally indebted to my family, as well as my dear friends Kyle Hays, Tim Treder, and Tom Burnett, who encouraged me to take my work in new directions while completing my MFA at Oklahoma State University. I owe a tremendous thanks to Timothy Liu for supporting my work and helping to shape several of these poems. I also want to thank Kirun Kapur for selecting this manuscript as the winner of the Elixir Press Antivenom Poetry Award.

There are no words to express the amount I've learned about writing and living from Clayton Dillard and Elliott Kastner.

And to my wife Ashley, I want to thank you for your tireless support and care. I love you.

Finally, I extend much gratitude to the editors of these literary journals, in which the following poems, often in different form, first appeared:

- *Backlash Journal:* "Getting By"
- *Black Fox:* "Small Continuous Explosions," "Forms of Interiority"

- *The Boiler:* "Genesis Litany" (excerpts)
- *Booth:* "Better Weather"
- *The Helix:* "Health and Vandalism" (excerpts)
- *The Journal:* "To My Dead Neighbor"
- *The McNeese Review:* "Last Street in the South" (originally published as "Street Hassle in the South"), "A Material World" (originally published as "Always Familiar")
- *Monarch Review:* "Last Call," "Local History"
- *Midway:* "Super 8" (originally published as "Chicago Revisited")
- *Off the Coast:* "The Chemicals in Our Veins Speak in Pleasant Voices" (excerpts)
- *Otis Nebula:* "Ordinary Moon" (excerpts)
- *Portland Review:* "Green Burial" (originally published as "In the Dustlight, Listen")
- *The Rush:* "The One You Like the Most"
- *Salt Hill:* "Health and Vandalism" (excerpts)
- *Sprung Formal:* "Love and Theft and the Airport" (excerpts)
- *Spry:* "Genesis Litany" (excerpts)
- *Tulsa Review:* "Houses Filled With People Who Resemble Other People"
- *Watershed Review:* "There Are No Birds in My House"
- *Word Riot:* "Sacrifice Zones" (originally published as "Similar Haircuts")
- *Yemassee:* "Apocalypse Litany" (excerpts)

Kameron Richardson

DEREK GRAF was born in Tampa, FL. He completed.his MFA at Oklahoma State University and his PhD at the University of Kansas. He currently lives in New York City. *Green Burial* is his first collection.

Poetry Titles from Elixir Press

Circassian Girl by Michelle Mitchell-Foust
Imago Mundi by Michelle Mitchell-Foust
Distance From Birth by Tracy Philpot
Original White Animals by Tracy Philpot
Flow Blue by Sarah Kennedy
A Witch's Dictionary by Sarah Kennedy
The Gold Thread by Sarah Kennedy
Rapture by Sarah Kennedy
Monster Zero by Jay Snodgrass
Drag by Duriel E. Harris
Running the Voodoo Down by Jim McGarrah
Assignation at Vanishing Point by Jane Satterfield
Her Familiars by Jane Satterfield
The Jewish Fake Book by Sima Rabinowitz
Recital by Samn Stockwell
Murder Ballads by Jake Adam York
Floating Girl (Angel of War) by Robert Randolph
Puritan Spectacle by Robert Strong
X-testaments by Karen Zealand
Keeping the Tigers Behind Us by Glenn J. Freeman
Bonneville by Jenny Mueller
State Park by Jenny Mueller
Cities of Flesh and the Dead by Diann Blakely
Green Ink Wings by Sherre Myers
Orange Reminds You Of Listening by Kristin Abraham
In What I Have Done & What I Have Failed To Do by Joseph P. Wood
Bray by Paul Gibbons
The Halo Rule by Teresa Leo
Perpetual Care by Katie Cappello
The Raindrop's Gospel: The Trials of St. Jerome and St. Paula by Maurya Simon
Prelude to Air from Water by Sandy Florian
Let Me Open You A Swan by Deborah Bogen

Cargo by Kristin Kelly
Spit by Esther Lee
Rag & Bone by Kathryn Nuerenberger
Kingdom of Throat-stuck Luck by George Kalamaras
Mormon Boy by Seth Brady Tucker
Nostalgia for the Criminal Past by Kathleen Winter
I will not kick my friends by Kathleen Winter
Little Oblivion by Susan Allspaw
Quelled Communiqués by Chloe Joan Lopez
Stupor by David Ray Vance
Curio by John A. Nieves
The Rub by Ariana-Sophia Kartsonis
Visiting Indira Gandhi's Palmist by Kirun Kapur
Freaked by Liz Robbins
Looming by Jennifer Franklin
Flammable Matter by Jacob Victorine
Prayer Book of the Anxious by Josephine Yu
flicker by Lisa Bickmore
Sure Extinction by John Estes
Selected Proverbs by Michael Cryer
Rise and Fall of the Lesser Sun Gods by Bruce Bond
Barnburner by Erin Hoover
Live from the Mood Board by Candice Reffe
Deed by Justin Wymer
Somewhere to Go by Laurin Becker Macios
If We Had a Lemon We'd Throw It and Call That the Sun by Christopher Citro
White Chick by Nancy Keating
The Drowning House by John Sibley Williams
Green Burial by Derek Graf
When Your Sky Runs into Mine by Rooja Mohassessy

Fiction Titles from Elixir Press

How Things Break by Kerala Goodkin
Juju by Judy Moffat
Grass by Sean Aden Lovelace
Hymn of Ash by George Looney
The Worst May Be Over by George Looney
Nine Ten Again by Phil Condon
Memory Sickness by Phong Nguyen
Troglodyte by Tracy DeBrincat

The Loss of All Lost Things by Amina Gautier
The Killer's Dog by Gary Fincke
Everyone Was There by Anthony Varallo
The Wolf Tone by Christy Stillwell
Tell Me, Signora by Ann Harleman
Far West by Ron Tanner
Out of Season by Kirk Wilson